THE CONTRARIAN VOICE

and

Other Poems

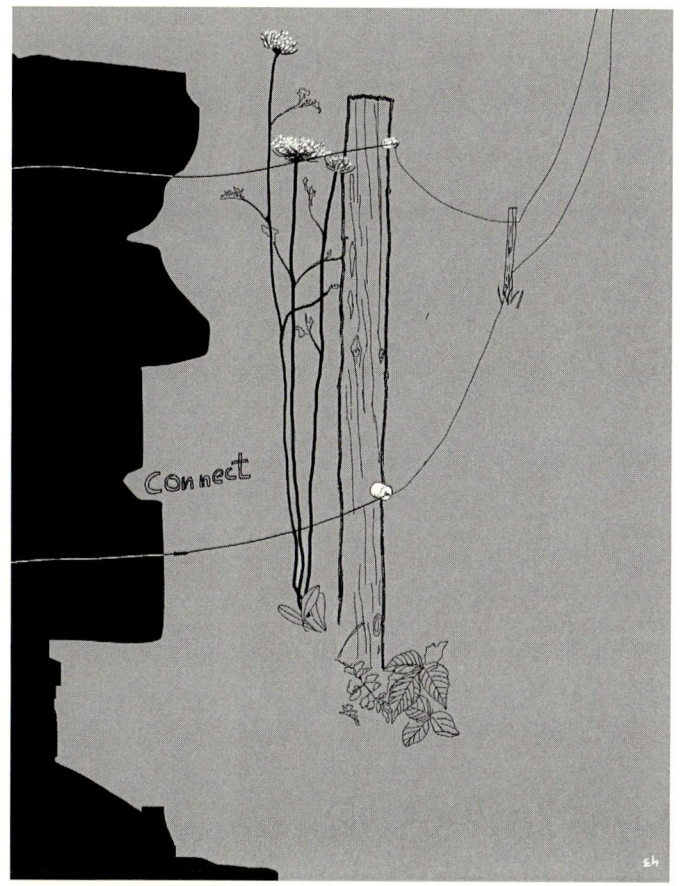

Ernest Hebert

BAUHAN PUBLISHING
Peterborough, New Hampshire
2017

Library of Congress Cataloging-in-Publication Data
Names: Hebert, Ernest, author.
Title: The contrarian voice : and other poems / by Ernest Hebert.
Description: First edition. | Peterborough, New Hampshire :
Bauhan Publishing, 2017.
Identifiers: LCCN 2017033105 (print) | LCCN 2017039111 (ebook) |
ISBN 9780872332492 (ebook) | ISBN 9780872332485 (softcover :
acid-free paper)
Classification: LCC PS3558.E277 (ebook) | LCC PS3558.E277 A6
2017 (print) |
DDC 811/.54--dc23LC record available at https://lccn.loc.
gov/2017033105

Book design by Sarah Bauhan
Cover design by Henry James
Typeset in Michael Harvey's Mentor, with Strayhorn titles
Illustrations and cover art by Ernest Hebert

BAUHAN
PUBLISHINGLLC
PO BOX 117 PETERBOROUGH NEW HAMPSHIRE 03458
603-567-4430
WWW.BAUHANPUBLISHING.COM
Follow us on Facebook and Twitter – @bauhanpub
MANUFACTURED IN THE UNITED STATES OF AMERICA

For Medora

CONTENTS

Note on the Title   9

I - Septuagenarian Look-Back

1941–   13
The Dogs of Tunapuna   14
You—We   15
To Do   18
Road Trip Note   20
Retirement Relocation?   21
Fricative Refract   23
Destination: Blivit City   24
A Tad   25
Everything Else . . .   26
A Writer's Melancholy Baby   27
Listening for the Soothing Sound   29
My Mother's Donuts   31

II - Poems Inspired by The God Roar

Hypothermia   35
The God Roar   37
Mad Boy and Miss Watson   38
Coydogs   41
Brother's Blood   42
It   45
Intimacy   46
Another You   47

III - Poems and Songs in the Darby Chronicles

Ocean Blues in Plenty   51
Emily's Song   52
Paintings   54
Bare Essentials   55
Praise the Road   56
Nowhere   57
The Dogs of March   58
(Untitled)   62
(Untitled)   63
Testimony   64
Interstices Between Dark Matter and Us   65
The Only Friend I Got   67

IV - Howard Elman: An Old Working Man's Meditations

Road Fare   71
The Orc Lass   73
Words from a Dead Language   75
Hell   77
Plow Guy's Lament   79
The Contrarian Voice   81

Acknowledgments   94

Note on the Title

I got the idea of *The Contrarian Voice* upon completion of my novel Howard Elman's Farewell. From there I started writing poems with the idea of a voice speaking somewhere in the head of my character Howard Elman. It soon occurred to me that this voice actually is in all my books. That's how it goes with me: the discoveries I make, such as they are, come in the writing I do, sometimes when I'm composing, but more often afterward. Discovery is my reason for writing, for drawing, for sculpting, for road-tripping, and even for conversing. I can't put it any better than May Sarton in her memoir *Journal of a Solitude*: "I have written every poem, every novel, for the same purpose—to find out what I think, to know where I stand." Just where do I stand? I think it is in the title piece of this collection.

I

SEPTUAGENARIAN
LOOK-BACK

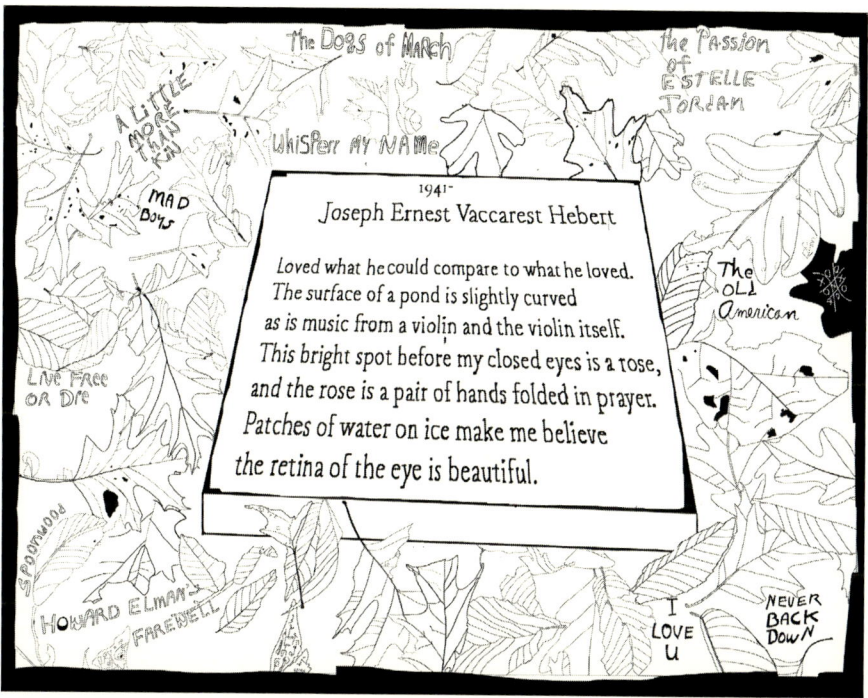

The Dogs of March

the Passion of ESTELLE TORJAN

A LITTLE MORE THAN KIN

Whisper MY NAMe

MAD Boys

The OLD American

Live FREE OR Die

Spoonwood

HOWARD ELMAN'S FAREWELL

I LOVE U

NEVER BACK DOWN

1941-
Joseph Ernest Vaccarest Hebert

Loved what he could compare to what he loved.
The surface of a pond is slightly curved
as is music from a violin and the violin itself.
This bright spot before my closed eyes is a rose,
and the rose is a pair of hands folded in prayer.
Patches of water on ice make me believe
the retina of the eye is beautiful.

1941-
Joseph Ernest Vaccarest Hebert

I loved what I could compare to what I loved.
The surface of a pond is slightly curved
as is music from a violin and the violin itself.
This bright spot before my closed eyes is a rose,
and the rose is a pair of hands folded in prayer.
Patches of water on ice make me believe
the retina of the eye is beautiful.

(A version of this work appeared in Volume 1, Number 1,
Summer 1975 Apple Tree Review, issued by a one-man
publishing house operated by my friend James T. Dunn.)

The Dogs of Tunapuna, Trinidad

The streets are full of them,
big-balled dogs with torn-up flanks
and limping bitches with prominent tits.
They sleep the day and roam the night
to mate, quarrel, and carry on.
For a couple hours you hear
only an occasional bark or yelp,
then all of a sudden half a dozen will start in.
Soon the entire island is howling.
It all sounds comic,
until you realize that these creatures
are killing and maiming one another
over useless territory and loveless fucking,
just like the rest of us,
a response to evolution,
spittle from the God Roar.

You—We

You're West Indian, we're North American.
We pity your three-legged bitches
with their stretched tits from too many puppies.
We admire the big balls of your dogs.
We cut the balls off our dogs so they don't breed,
nor embarrass us with their public carnality.
We love our dogs neutered,
which basically is how we prefer our friends
because they are less dangerous with no balls.
You regard your dogs as little guard folks.
What are you afraid of, Trinidadians—with your
pit bulls, security guards, concrete barriers,
barbed wire fences, and steel-barred gates?
You say, bandits, but we don't believe it.
You are afraid of something else—what is it?

We are not afraid of bandits.
Our most admired movies are about bandits.
The Godfather is considered a classic.
Imagine that. Another of our classics,
The Great Gatsby, is about worthless hangers-on
and maybe an admirable bandit—
hard to tell, the character is not developed.
If Gatsby were not rich we would not admire him.
We only admire rich bandits.

When we catch a poor bandit, we execute him;
we never execute rich bandits.
We despise and persecute the poor
even when they are not bandits.
Are things so different here?

You say you are multicultural—
African, East Indian, Chinese—
but from your behavior you seem, like us,
more shamed English than anything else.
We're appalled by your gray water ditches,
but if you saw our college fraternity basements
where young men piss against the walls and everyone
gets drunk and says they're having a good time,
you'd . . . you'd . . . well,
we don't know what you'd do,
because, really, we don't know you.
We don't care to know you.
We want you to know us.

We don't know why you walk so slow and drive so fast.
We scurry and scamper; you saunter and stroll.
Our beggars work the exit ramps and intersections.
Your beggars accost me on the street.
"Now that the sun has darkened my skin,
I can pass, so why do beggars still mistake me
for a tourist with money?" I ask my wife.

"Because you don't walk like a Trinidadian."
I feel comfortable here
since I learned to drive fast and walk slow.
The driving takes concentration.
The walking takes concentration.
I try to keep my crooked back straight,
and swing my arms gently, and think with each step.

To Do

Start small fire of dry hemlock twigs.
Add bigger sticks.
Straddle fire with grill.
Scoop snow into pot, place on grill.
Watch snow melt, first to slush,
then to water.
Bits of the forest will be in the water.
No such thing as pure snow, pure water.
Water always contains
something other than itself.
Water is the primal container.
Bring water to boil.
Drop in tea bag.
Remove pot from flame
and place on flat stone.
Watch water darken.
Observe colors and reflections.
Remove tea bag, squeeze out water,
throw bag in fire.
Watch fire consume tea bag.
Observe flames and smoke.
Kick grill over,
watch hot metal cut snow.
Pick up grill, heat gone from it.
Wipe and return to pack.

Place more sticks in fire.
Pour tea into cup.
Listen to the near chatter of the fire
in counterpoint to the far whisper
of the falling snow.
Bring cup to lips, tongue.

Road Trip Note

First day on the road is an up day.
Septuagenarian is excited and optimistic.
Day two belongs to Voice
who reminds me of my failures,
cowardly acts, stupid remarks,
and so forth through piles of miles.
On day three distance substitutes
for memory and Voice goes silent.
All Septuagenarian knows is the road.
The trip begins.

Retirement Relocation?

I liked the isolation,
liked the lazy lagoon,
liked the fishing boats
in their little water cubbies
in the man-made harbor,
liked my fellow retirees,
their pauses before speaking,
liked the redfish served breaded
and cooked in boiling oil.
Buy a nice mobile home
here in the local trailer park
and maybe, just maybe,
have enough left over to buy a boat.
Imagine that—a boat
for local ocean travel.
Anchored out
writing poems, catching redfish,
musing.
Eat the local oranges
that grow on trees.
Imagine that—oranges grow
on trees in South Texas.
Pick an orange from a tree
in my yard. Can't do that in NH.
Eat the local cows

cooked on mesquite fires.
A joy to walk the gravel flats
of the Laguna Madre to watch birds:
in place of regrets, egrets.
Sing it like Sinatra:
Egrets, I've had a few
but too few to mention.
Septuagenarian waiting to die
in Port Mansfield, Texas.
Almost convinced myself to stay.

Fricative Refract

The act has to be physical
as well as mental.
Lips must move.
Tongue must waggle.
Teeth grind.
Eyes tear up.
Mouth widen with smile
or fall with frown.
Facial muscles animate with feeling.
In the car–out loud.
On the street–a whisper.
Before sleep–captions
underneath the mind-video.
When I talk to myself.

Destination: Blivit City

Forgetfulness is the ultimate blessing
for the demented and the dead.
Unless you are religious,
in which case you are confronted
at the gates by Saint Peter
or some other asshole
holding a ledger of your sins
who will remind you
there are places to go
after death besides oblivion.
Like Blivit City.
Blivit? What's a blivit?
A blivit is ten pounds of you
in a five-pound bag of Faith.
"I'm just gathering the evidence,"
Saint Peter will say, "God is the judge."
Why should God give a flaming fuck
what my sins are?
Doesn't he have enough to do
without bothering us septuagenarians?

A Tad

For some people a writing exercise is a seed that they can plant and grow creative work out of. Me, I never worked from an exercise in my life. Writers—we're all different in the way we go about dreaming up our pieces and setting down the words. What we have in common is that we perceive ourselves as outsiders. Most of us work alone, and most of us are at the core uncomfortable in our relations with our fellow human beings. We watch them, but we are never quite among them. It's easy for writers to become isolated because isolation is inherent in our nature. For that reason we need to come together once in a while. We need to remind ourselves that writers for better and for worse shaped the world, from the Declaration of Independence to Mein Kampf, from ads in magazines to suicide notes. Remember that God didn't write his own stuff in the Bible and the Koran and all those other good books. The prophets were His ghostwriters. All writing is important, even the stuff you never show anyone, because every line helps you understand yourself a tad better. A tad? What is a tad? Is a tad more or less than an iota, bigger or smaller than a smidgen? It's only writers who ask themselves such seemingly unimportant questions.

Everything Else . . .

There is no afterlife.
There is the beforelife,
which we gain from books, pictures,
and stories that our elders tell,
and, who knows, some remnant event
from an ancestor's trauma
passed down into our DNA.
Just how much of the self
is in the DNA I don't know.
Do things matter that you don't know?
Not to me they don't.
There is memory–
all memory is false memory, you say.
So what? False memory is all anybody's got.
There is the life of the moment
as you, we, I apprehend it.
Everything else is rumor.
Which may not be true,
but it's a good starting point
for writing your novel.

A Writer's Melancholy Baby

When my baby is rejected
I hurt but I don't mourn.
I send my baby out again.
I live on writer-hope for publication,
which is like waving down a stranger
to give you mouth-to-mouth resuscitation,
gross, if necessary.
When nobody will publish my baby
I give up and retire it to a shelf.
Writer-hope is still in me, if downgraded,
like the head of a dead loved one in a freezer—
who knows, maybe in some future time
it can be infused and come back to life—
which is why I pray for the soul
of my childhood idol, Ted Williams.

Or, lucky me, I find an editor who likes it
and my baby is published. Oh, happy day!
Actually, happy twenty minutes
because pretty quick I'm depressed
because I realize my baby has left home
and belongs to the readers now.
I wish I could forget my baby but I can't.
I feel pride or anger, depending on the treatment
of my baby—admired, scorned, ignored—

ignored is the worst, which makes me realize
writing to publish is just trying to get attention.
Inner Voice says: Write for money, Ernie,
so you don't have to write self-pitying shit like this.
But, Inner Voice, I have no talent for writing for money.

Muse says:
Services for the dead help us mourn together,
but when your book goes out of print
there is no service, no obituary.
Only you care when your baby dies,
because to everybody else it's not a baby,
it's just a book.
If you see it for sale in a used bookstore
you have an uplifting Lazarus moment
until you learn the price, 90 cents.
You laugh in horror—
your baby is now a zombie.
All that remains of value
is that special kind of hurt in mourning alone.
I give you permission, Ernie, to write this shit
and, haha, call it a poem.

Listening for the Soothing Sound

Sounds muted in life are raucous in memory.
The nun with the clapper
at St. Joe's prepared me
for the hut-horp of the Army
parade field. "Hippo-hoppo
who got the moppo?" sang
the drill sergeant.
"Your left . . . your left . . .
your left right left."
I loved the echo.
Good sounds but, really,
not so soothing.
In New York waking at 3 a.m.
I heard the radio static
left over from the Big Bang.
At Wallis Sands Beach the sound
of the waves crashing on the rocks
consecrated my love for you.
When I heard that first baby's
first laugh I realized I'd heard
the sound of home:
responsibility, commitment,
the death of what I thought
I really wanted–freedom.
Today, deaf, I don't even want that.

It's not quiet in my head. The tinnitus
mixes up echoes, Big Bangs,
and laughing babies tinni-trip
into a barely discernible hiss.
Without the hearing aid
there is no difference in the sound
of *deaf* and *death*.
One night I hear it in memory,
the soothing sound,
from my boyhood on 19 Oak Street
in Keene, New Hampshire,
my mother working at her foot-operated
Singer brand sewing machine.

My Mother's Donuts

On your deathbed
you told me the stems
of the flowers I picked for you
when I was a boy
were too short to put in a vase.
"I didn't have the heart
to tell you," you said.
I remembered the smell of the sun
on my clothes that you hung
on the line on a hot summer day.
And in the winter the smell of the air
from the clothes
steaming off the radiators.
You remembered how happy you were
with a new electric dryer.
I remembered you made donuts,
the aroma, the heavenly taste
when the donut
is still hot from the boiling oil.
By the time they cooled
the taste was ordinary.
"In those days people didn't tie
their dogs," you said.
"Yes, they came from miles around
drawn by the smell of your donuts.

You always made the mistake
of throwing them the holes."
"I couldn't help myself."
I laughed—you were too weak to laugh.
"And in the spring
when Dad burned the dead grasses,
do you remember that smell?
And the color of the new grass
growing through the black burn scar
after the rain, the brightest green
of the new season?"
There's no waiting for an answer;
you've shut your eyes.
I go back in time,
see myself picking flowers,
a boy's pure love for his mother,
so brief.

II

POEMS INSPIRED BY
The God Roar
(A NOVEL I NEVER WROTE,
WHICH IN TURN WAS INSPIRED
BY A SCULPTURE BY
BRENDA GARAND)

Hypothermia

I saw what I thought was that old self,
a snow mogul throbbing with a heartbeat,
human being as sculpture.
But that was not the old me after all.
It was you,
not dead, but like one pretending to be dead,
body temperature dangerously low,
mind not exactly unconscious, in a torpor.
I stripped you to your underwear.
You were slender with small breasts,
a boyish ass, and a curved feminine belly.
I undressed, leaving on only my shorts.
Crawled into the sleeping bag with you,
and looked at the Big Dipper through hardwoods
bare of leaves. Slowly you began
to warm up. "Come to consciousness," I said.
"Do I know you?" you said.
"I hardly know myself," I said.
We lay quiet and still for an hour,
then I asked why you came into these woods.
You said, "Listen."
"I don't hear anything."
"Yes you do–listen."
"I hear it now,
the tick and scrape of tree branches."

"How nice when the wind blows through the tops
of the trees and underneath it's still."
"You came for that, a sound?"
"Yes, the God Roar, to record it for posterity.
I heard Him in that sharp, cold wind
and lay down to die in the snow.
He was kind to me; I heard Him whisper,
'Don't be afraid.'
I heard Him when he brushed the snow off me."
"That wasn't God, that was me."
"No, it was God. You were doing his bidding."
"You were listening to God and forgot you were cold."
"Maybe not, maybe He planned it knowing
you would save me and bring us together.
Understand?"
"How can I
when my first thought was you were a snow mogul?"
"You're thinking of me as a problem
when actually I'm a solution."

The God Roar

We supped on homemade bread and lentil soup
flavored with garlic, onion, carrot, and potato,
eaten with wooden spoons I'd carved from white birch.
You said, "I like these spoons; no clinking sounds."
"I never thought about the sounds before."
"If you listen, you can entertain yourself
with just about any sound."
"So everything is music?"
"Everything waits to be made into music."
"That's where you come in with your recorder."
"I hope so, yes. The soup was delicious—thank you."
You pushed the wooden bowl aside.
"Do you serve meat?" you asked.
"Not since the middle of the summer
when I found the deer herd, my family."
"I'm glad you don't eat meat."
"Do you eat meat?" I asked.
"When I have to—I've always wanted to eat lion,
not the flesh, the roar. God is in that roar,
begging for me to eat Him and relieve His despair."

Mad Boy and Miss Watson

We walked through the softening snow of a warm,
false spring day in search of the deer herd,
but we couldn't find it.
I guessed that the Family, what was left of it,
had moved to the next hill where there was more cover.
"You must hate hunters," you said.
"No, I respect hunters. They really care about the deer.
They'll work hard to maintain the herds."
"But for their own purposes, deaths of particular deer."
"Hunters, like gods, do things for their own purposes
without guilt or self-reflecting analysis;
maybe that's why I admire them,
because they're constitutionally not like me."
"I don't think that's the reason."
You stopped before you hurt me
by voicing the thing we were both thinking.

Under the heat of a double-crossing, early-spring sun,
a misplaced stream of tropical air,
on cold ground still wet with melted snow,
we fucked like wild runaway teenagers. For me
it was like getting off the bus, home at last.

"I want to tell you the story again, okay?" I asked.
"They say every time you retrieve a memory,
you damage it."

"Yes, that's why I want to tell it. Again.
After my abuser had tired of me and tried to kill me
and I'd escaped alone, naked but free,
I'd searched for a somebody in myself
that I could love, an inverse Huck Finn.
Huck was a kid who'd discovered the pleasures
of freedom and fought to hold on, hold on barely,
by running away from women and home."
"And taking up with a Jim."
"Yes, and like Huck, I had freedom thrust upon me;
my fight was not to escape—did that—
but to confine myself to one place, one woman.
As much as Huck wanted to get away from Miss Watson,
I wanted to find her and fuck her blind.
And now I have. You make me feel religious.
It's a miracle, Miss Watson."
"Don't call me Miss Watson, call me Jim."
"The man who had taken me with him
cross-country in a van when I was a boy
liked to see me naked. But he never
touched me. He only made me look at him,
except at the decisive moment and then he'd
turn away so I couldn't see his face.
He'd make a noise like a pained gargle
that gave me a little thrill as if, really,

I owned him. We bedded down on a big mattress
that took up the greater part of the van.
He'd handcuff my right hand to a metal ring,
and then he'd sleep, restless and thrashing;
I would masturbate with the free hand,
replaying scenes between us, except in my mind
now I was the abuser, in my place another figure—
not boy, not man, not woman, not girl,
but a sculpture by Brenda Garand.
I wanted to fuck it, and it me. The end.
What do you think of my story?"
"Let's make love again," you said.
I would tell you the story in different ways
and we would make love in different ways;
then, inspired, we would both work on our art,
me carving sticks, you recording the sounds
in our woods for your disturbing podcasts.

Coydogs

On one of the coldest nights of the winter,
you woke me. "Listen," you said.
I heard it, faint, but distinct and piercing.
"Coydogs," I said.
"That's right. I want to get closer."
We dressed and went out into the night, air still,
sounds of our footfalls on crispy snow
like a clenched fist crushing an idea,
so cold that as we exhaled
our breath froze into moonglow-colored flower petals,
like a question full of dependent clauses.
"Follow the sounds," you said.
"They're everywhere," I said.
"No, only two."
We saw the coydogs on a ledge
where the wind had swept away
most of the snow. They stood twenty feet apart.
One would howl at the indifferent moon,
then the other. You ran the recorder.
"This is what I came here for," you said.
I thought: After this night she will leave me.
One made one last call to the moon,
then lifted her rear end and gave it a shake.
We watched them mate, sounds softer now and pained,
as if they knew that a satisfied yearning
only gives way to another.
Afterward, they went their separate ways.

Brother's Blood

I passed the time by following a young doe
and her companion, a spikehorn buck.
I called her sister, and I called him brother.
They were on the outs with the herd,
or so I imagined. The rut season ruined
their innocence and got me to thinking
that I'd been out here too long.
I went looking for my deer for solace,
but God, the sculptor,
after participating in the orgy of the herd,
worked on his art by making snow fall.
I looked up and said, "Behold."
When I looked down again, the tracks were gone.

A brook slinked upward through a gorge;
above it the land was gentler.
Here had once been a farm, grown over now.
I guessed the deer would break off from the brook
where the land flattened out.
It didn't take long before I was lost.
More than an inch of snow had fallen over my tracks.
And then I stumbled upon an apple tree,
a magnificent piece of God,
both young-growing and dead-dying at the same time,
the kind of thing I would make

if I had Brenda Garand's powers.
Hoofs had disturbed the ground only minutes ago.

Then I heard the sharp crack of a rifle
that shook snow from a hemlock down my neck
and chilled me. I could see blaze orange ahead.
I watched from behind a tree as two men hunched
over my fallen brother. One was holding a knife,
making an incision along the belly.
"Nice little spikehorn."
"You lucky bastid—me, I'll wait for a big buck."
"You're welcome to it. Meat on the young is sweeter."
"The other one got away."
"I don't think so—I think I got her. Two for one."
"Not in the rule book."
"Yah, right. The freezer don't care."
"Anyway, I don't believe you got her."
"We'll hang this one up, and go look for blood.
We'll find her. You can bet on it."
Brother's guts spilled steaming onto the snow,
and then the man lifted brother up for the other man
to look at. "I figure he'll go about 150 pounds."
"More like 110—haha."
I didn't feel anything at the time,
just detached from myself, a little queasy.

I went looking for sister's blood, but I didn't see any.
I really didn't want to find sister.
What could I do for her when I was really looking
for that you I found dying in a snowbank?
The loss of brother told me how crazy and desperate
my recent life had been. A man searching
for his family in a deer herd!
I wanted the deer to draw me out of my ambitions,
my lust, my almighty self.
But in the end it was hunters who did it.
How ennobling to my human condition.

It

After you left me,
I cruised the he/she bars and found another you.
We went to her place. I paid and said,
"You must make pretty good money
so why live in a cheap room like this?"
She cupped a silicone breast. "Don't you get IT?"
"You're stashing every dollar for a silicone valley."
She smiled, in affirmation I thought at first,
but I was wrong.
"Won't you miss IT?" I asked.
"Without the excess, I can be the perfect woman."
"Even if science can help, isn't IT tragic?
I mean, how long can you remain 'perfect'–
six months, a year, maybe two, five at the most?"
"I don't think about IT; I think about becoming."
"Is that b-e-c-u-m-m-i-n-g?"
"No jokes," she said. "Jokes kill the pleasure
of sex. You, what do you think about?"
She had me there. I started laughing and could not erect.

Intimacy

It was another week before I saw her again.
Another you. Always there is another you.
I broke the broom handle over my knee,
and let the pieces fall to the floor.
The violence of the gesture made her tremble.
I pulled the light cord out of the wall.
The lamp hadn't read the script
and fell on the floor, the ceramic base shattering.
The unscripted noise startled us both,
as if a stranger had wandered into our ritual,
and for a few seconds we were both embarrassed.
I returned to the script and cut the lamp cord.
"Please," I said, motioning for her to kneel.
I used the broom handle as a spreader
and tied her ankles. I smacked her ass
with my callused hand. Then we fucked briefly
and with dignity and a minimum of commotion
in the missionary position. I wanted to kiss her,
but intimacy was not in our script.

Another You

Probably it was better that I can't picture her.
Representations within memory,
whether of people or landscapes or simple objects,
wear out with the imagining;
abstractions might not satisfy as deeply,
might leave one unsettled, but they never wear out.
I looked over her smooth back
into a distance, a fog, a veil.
After the sex, I said, "I needed you tonight
a lot more than you needed me."
"Is that the truth?"
"The truth as I know it."
She took my callused hands.
"I think I get it," she said. "You have a day job.
You work with your hands. You're ashamed
to say what you do. It's all right, I won't ask."
She kissed my hands. Five minutes later I was gone.
I managed to control my urges until
I arrived at my studio.
I split a billet with my hatchet,
shaped apple wood with a two-handed knife
into a stick, notched the stick;
with a cord around the notch I
hung it up on the wall with a hundred others,
my lowly necessary art.

Made another. Another. Another.
It's only with hands
that I can feel a tree's potential.
By dawn, still awake but tired,
I thought about the other you,
how I had deceived her into believing
I was a working man and not a lowly whittler.
Then I was erecting;
then I was content.

III

POEMS AND SONGS
IN THE DARBY CHRONICLES

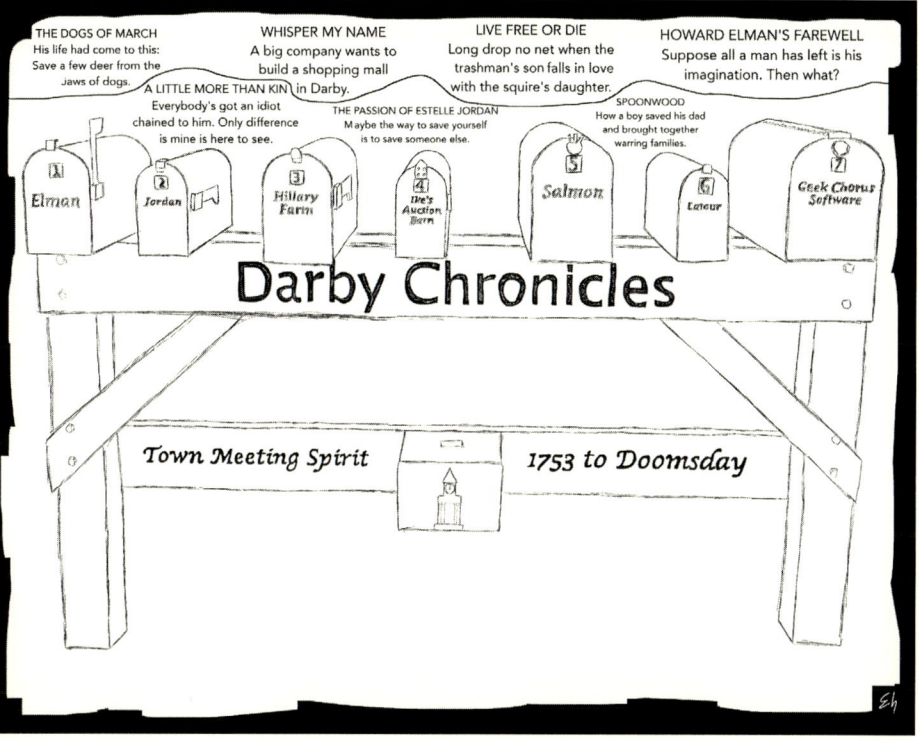

Ocean Blues in Plenty

Fears of scarcity seem like an ancient superstition.
Crowds shop instead of breaking windows.
Great rolls of time unravel. Only Darwin complains
that there is vengeance in a stool.
Philosophers favor memorial services for ideas over ideas.
A man named Edgar photographs poisoned fruit.
Darwin writhes. He has not found truth; truth has found him.

[This piece is attributed to Hadly Blue in my novel *A Little More
Than Kin*. I got the name Edgar from my friend Edgar Bernstein,
who was a photographer, and a good one, back in our college days.]

Emily's Song

The TV speaks to Emily in her rocking chair.
The Secret Storm rages and then subsides.
A woman confesses how she rid the chafe
from her hands.
      Roses for Emily.

Emily's waiting for *Love of Life* to come on the screen.
The sun has wilted her plants,
and the leaves are in mourning.
The wind tips the rocker first forward then back
and blows through her thin gray hair.
Outside, the cat yowls for the back door
to open itself.
      Roses for Emily.

She's waiting for *Love of Life* to come on the screen.
She always liked this room—the smell of the sofa
and sounds of the shade cord tapping on the window.
On the floor, years ago, played the Lieutenant boy
she lost in the war. On the lawn today, Mr. Robin bobs
for a worm, like a fine gentleman
tipping his cap.
      Roses for Emily.

Emily's waiting for *Love of Life* to come on the screen.
The wind carries the fragrance of flowers inside,
to linger by her rocker, like an oarsman pausing
to watch the sea. The neighborhood is napping;
children lie softly as fur. The rower dipping
his oar, first in the water and then the sun,
the insistent cat, the flowers teasing the wind,
the robin and his great dignity; the children,
even the woman with the chafed heart
have what Emily had until three o'clock. *The Secret Storm*
has ended and *Love of Life* comes on the screen.
        Roses for Emily, roses for Emily, roses.

[This song, which appears in *A Little More Than Kin*, was inspired by
Fritz Bernstein one day while she sang a song and played her guitar on
Central Square in Keene, New Hampshire, in (I think) 1980.]

Paintings

Places I have never seen
that perhaps no longer exist
or have never existed—
muddied oils of New England villages
by unknown artists which can be had
cheap at country auctions—
might be places to go
if they drop the bomb
or if the world were to go suddenly, permanently
bonkers
or if you leave me.

[These lines were attributed to Hadly Blue in *Whisper My Name*.]

Bare Essentials

Cash to pay my way, wheels to carry me.
In place of destination a direction: West.
All day and into the night—West.
Across the land—West.
Across the waters—West.
Butterfly stroke to Hawaii—West.
Breast stroke to Japan—West.
No, now West brings us to the Far East.
How can far West equal Far East?
Is it any wonder I'm so screwed up?
Faster I run, faster I'm back where I started from.
North, freeze, becomes South, fry;
West, freedom, becomes East, creation.
To hell with these laws,
I'll live by my law: West forever.
Straight to the end of everything.
Live Free or Die,
you're all I got for home.

[Attributed to Frederick Elman, a.k.a. F. Latour, in *Live Free or Die*.]

Praise the Road

I stay on back roads to avoid police,
real and imaginary.
I listen to the Christian minister on the radio
and look at the scenery.
A wood-frame schoolhouse
has been converted into a chiropractic center.
Praise the Lord.

Aching backs, arthritic joints, venereal sores,
cancerous tumors, AIDS kisses, broken hearts,
busted humps—pain and mortality—why, yes,
I understand now what it's all about,
the world not round but inside out,
a Möbius strip dangling like a decoration
in the waiting room of a chiropractic center.
Praise the Lord.

If I ain't good at living,
what's the use of living?
If I'm no good to me and thee,
what's the Good?
They'll say he drove too fast.
They'll say he jumped the rail.
At road's end, they'll say, man and vehicle
took holy communion with a telephone pole.
Praise the Lord.

[Attributed to Frederick Elman, a.k.a. F. Latour, in *Live Free or Die*.]

Nowhere

Whip off the main road
onto a road without a name sign or number
then off onto another road.
Lose yourself.
Go nowhere, sleep nowhere, wake nowhere.
In the morning, drive away from the sun,
from nowhere to now, here.

[Attributed to Frederick Elman, a.k.a. F. Latour, in *Live Free or Die*. I added the last line. Sorry, Freddy, I couldn't resist.]

The Dogs of March

My feet sting with cold—
"His feet sting with cold,"
the choir mocks him in song—
the back of my trigger hand is numb and blue;
my nose runs, I weep.
"This is no hunter, providing food for family and tribe.
This fellow confuses police tactics with religion,
exercise with duty. He's just a man with a gun."
I listen for the crackle of disturbed leaves,
hear only the crunch of my own footfalls.
I scan the measures between trees.
I search for a movement, a flash of white light.
She's there. I sense her, delicate, unaware.

Snow begins to fall,
as if it had been falling in a time before this,
I a self before this self.
The gray whitens, less a cloak,
more a sheath to protect the blade of the new season.
I cut the distance between us. Downwind
I wait, patient, stiff;
my scent crouches in the rocks like a bad memory.
"Mocking himself, he mocks us all.
Disinter his bones and put him in the movies."
I hear her. Hoofs stroke the snow,

Soft mouth nuzzles the tips of the hemlock trees.
My neck is sopping with frigid dew,
and I am cold but do not shiver.
The rifle warms me, squares my shoulders,
drops me to one knee. I am in perfect position.
I feel like a dancer.
My vision narrows to a point of white light.
A string tightens from a place inside me.
The noise goes slack, then comes round in echo.
I rise to my feet and follow the bullet.

Snow forms flesh on the bones of the trees.
It falls as if in a time before this,
to pay homage to a time before that.
It falls with the grace of a penitent
dropping to his knees.
The doe has no vision of coming winter,
no vision of the dogs of March,
their paws skimming along the hard rough crust
while her sharp hoofs plunge through.
A dancer, suddenly awkward, alone, pursued,
she listens to her breath.

She sees shades of gray over shades of gray.
The trails she follows are marked by their smell,

wind down into nodes,
where remembrance of sleep lies softly as fur.
Her ears are cocked like an audience's,
her nerve endings choir singers
listening for their cues.
It is then the horizon joins the earth,
and becomes moss.
Is this sharp awareness a color? Is color a curve
like a boat, and she rising to the surface to meet it,
rising to meet the horizon,
rising from the dark depths of oily waters, rising,
breaking through to the broad lake?
Or only the snow pressing against the leaves?

The bright color of flesh colors the snow.
She begins to fall slowly to her knees,
then she rises while a part of her does not rise.
Her nerve endings jerk spasmodically.
She crashes through brush,
the strings of her body pulling all wrong and violently.

"In pursuit, he hears a pounding on the forest floor,
which is the sound of his own footfalls
mingled with the sound of his crazy dreams.
He hears his child bang without purpose
on an organ in an empty church."

She falls and is still. I find her.
I unsheathe my knife and open her belly,
leaving her insides steaming on new snow.
I curse, my lips crack when I try to speak,
and my hands blister when I reach for her.
I drag the body across the orchard.
The falling snow gently heals the bruised earth
with its nothingness.

[Attributed to Frederick Elman, a.k.a. F. Latour, in *Live Free or Die*. I
made a couple of minor changes.]

(Untitled)

The sea in her gift for composition
has a made a place, if not a self,
for that rock, that kelp.
Thus I am unconcerned
that my hat has blown away,
that the gulls are laughing:
"There is less of him than usual."

[Attributed to Hadly Blue in *A Little More Than Kin*.]

(Untitled)

Father, accept my sacrifice
of these two pears.
I will tie them in a loose bag
to hang from this branch.
They will turn soft and sweet
changing gender as does a season.

[Attributed to Hadly Blue in *A Little More Than Kin*.]

Testimony

We bend to our knees,
scoop up the water and drink it.
We remember the cold on our skin,
the taste on our tongues,
the tactile feel
as the water goes down our throats.
Later, when we stand before our friends,
or perhaps the jury, we say,
"I held the river in my hands."

[Attributed to Frederick Elman, a.k.a. F. Latour, in *Howard Elman's Farewell*.]

Interstices Between Dark Matter and Us

I put my son in the front-pack baby carrier
for a walk in the woods, headed for Grace Pond.
What do you see, boy?
I read his answer in the thought he sends me.
Spiderwebs in ferns, in trees, in the interstices
between the comet dust that makes up
the rings of Saturn
and the loved one who left us too early.
Give me water, Father, give me water.
I tip a moose-wood leaf toward my son's mouth,
and droplets of dew quench his thirst.

When we reach Grace Pond I place the baby carrier
on the stern seat of the johnboat and tie it down.
I row out into the pond to the cove
full of lily pads and the gray skeletons
of dead pine trees rising out of the shallows
like big ideas that just don't work.
We've come to see the heron.
She walks on her stilt legs
until she finds a station.
She stands motionless waiting for the judgment.
I hold the oars so they don't part the waters.
My son sends me a thought.
I answer with my own thought:

I'm thinking of your mother, too.
The heron darts her beak into the water
and comes up with a yellow perch.
Fish crossways in her mouth, she begins
a laborious takeoff,
tucking her stilt legs behind her,
huge wings slapping water as she strains for a height,
finally rising on an air current,
circling back into the nest at the top of a dead pine.
I look through the binoculars
and see a chick's open mouth.
I let out a celebratory whoop.
My son throws up his hands and imitates my whoop,
his first word.

[Attributed to Frederick Elman, a.k.a. F. Latour, in *Howard Elman's Farewell*.]

The Only Friend I Got

Since you departed, darlin',
he's all I got for company,
that confused old man in the bathroom mirror.
They say the day I won't remember him
is the day I won't remember you,
so I treasure him—
he's the only friend I got.

They say he moves his lips
when he walks down the street.
They say he repeats himself,
they say he repeats himself,
and he misses when he shaves
and that's okay.
I say all he misses is you—
he's the only friend I got.

Remember when you did all the talking, darlin',
handled all the family trouble?
Remember those days, darlin',
when I checked the oil
and you wrote the checks?
I saw him this morning in that mirror—
the only friend I got.

He says, better put on your reading glasses—
if you can find them.
He looks at me, kinda puzzled,
kinda tired.
He says, we loved her, doncha know.
I nod and he nods.
I says to him I says,
you're the only friend I got,
all the rest are dead and gone.

They say he moves his lips
when he walks down the street.
They say he repeats himself,
they say he repeats himself.
They say he misses when he shaves
and that's okay.
I say he's the only friend I got
and all he misses is you
and all he misses is you
and all he misses is you.

[Song attributed to Tahoka Texas McCloud in *Howard Elman's Farewell*.]

IV

HOWARD ELMAN:
AN OLD WORKING MAN'S
MEDITATIONS

Road Fare

Pick up car-killed creatures
along the highways
for the Centenarian's stewpot—
birds of different feathers, coyotes,
deer, porcupines, woodchucks,
squirrels, muskrats, beavers,
raccoons (many raccoons),
perhaps a bear cub,
and even a fisher cat.
Please, no skunks.
Add vegetables
from grocery store dumpsters
and compost piles,
an occasional noodle or grain,
herbs with *h*'s removed, and salt
(as Leo Lavoie used to say,
not too much now).
Octogenarian laughs and says,
"You, me, we've gone
off the deep end."
"Deep end? End of what?"
The Centenarian seems
to ponder his phrase.
Then he repeats, "Deep end, end deep.
How deep is deep,

how far the end,
and where do we go from there?"
Smacking his lips
as if tasting the words,
but of course it is only stew.

The Orc Lass

The only person at this hour
in the town hall is the Orc Lass.
She's only maybe fifty,
but she acts seventy-five.
Which for you, Octogenarian,
is the attraction.
She refuses to use a computer
and types all the town business
on an ancient IBM Selectric typewriter.
I figure she's . . . what's that word
with the *tit* in it?
Titillated.
Yeah, that's the one,
sexually titillated by her power
to manipulate the ball
that strikes the platen.
Actually, it's you, Octogenarian,
who is titillated
watching her type.
You resist the urge to shout,
"Type my balls."
Orc Lass is one of those women
blessed with giant bazzooms.
She has a big frame,
wide all the way around,

grand hips, protruding ass,
shoulders like a sidewalk curb.
With her squared glasses
and drab gray dress
she looks like a cement truck
driving into the sun.
Yes, beautiful.

Words from a Dead Language

They sat around the tiny table,
Octogenarian and Centenarian eating stew,
Cyborg Lass and Dyslectic Cyborg Lad
sipping herb tea concoction.
Who put the *h* in *erb tea*?
"Hiss, hess, hoss," Dyslectic Cyborg Lad said,
as if speaking to his handheld.
"What are you studying?" Centenarian asked.
"The Latin language."
"When I was an altar boy,
we used to speak Latin in church."
"So, you could teach me Latin?"
asked Dyslectic Cyborg Lad.
"Can't; they didn't tell us
what the words meant.
What do you know so far?"
"Not too much; I just started.
Hiss, hess, hoss,
hew I us, hew I us, hew I us."
Cyborg Lass put in her two cents' worth:
"The correct pronunciation is
hick, hike, hock,
whoweeus, whoweeus, whoweeus,"
I think *huius* subs for Julius,
like Julius Caesar who

conquered much of the known world."
"He was probably compensating
for his sissy name," Octogenarian said.
Centenarian turned to Dyslectic Cyborg Lad:
"Me and Octogenarian,
we're hicks, so that's the hick part.
Hike could be like when you're playing
football and the quarterback says, 'Hike,'
or maybe it's like 'take a hike,'
and hock is like you leave something
at a pawnshop."
"Hock could also be a hunk of spit,"
Octogenarian said. He winked at Cyborg Lass
to confirm his humor.
"Put them together," Cyborg Lass said,
"hick, hike, hock could be translated
as 'Country boy pawns his football.'"
"Wouldn't that be
hick, hock, hike?" Dyslectic Cyborg Lad asked,
straight-faced, not kidding.
"By gosh, you're right," Centenarian said,
not kidding.

Hell

Octogenarian is thinking about the Devil,
which of course he does not believe in,
at least not strictly,
guy with horns sticking out
of his head and a tail.
Why would the Devil have a tail?
Balance?
If there is a Devil
he would not look like the Devil.
The Devil would be a smoothie;
he would look like Evil Selectman.
Octogenarian suddenly realizes that Evil Selectman
resembles that boring bandleader
Wife had a crush on.
Lawrence Welk!
You may or may not have to face
the Devil,
but you do have to face death.
Think about the possibilities.
In bed sleeping. Car crash.
Slo-mo and incapacitated
in a nursing home.
A fall.
Lost in the woods.
Lost in dementia.

Icepick in the ear.
Gunfight,
like John Wayne in *The Shootist.*
Squashed wrasslin' with the Orc Lass
in a giant bowl of Jell-O.
And the afterlife?
Saint Peter intrudes:
"For your sins, Octogenarian, for your sins:
strapped down in front of a TV."
What's on in my long tonight?
"Lawrence Welk band for all eternity."

Plow Guy's Lament

About six inches had fallen.
Nice little storm.
Junior was just finishing up
plowing out the driveway.
Octogenarian walked over to the truck.
Junior rolled down the window.
"How come you, not your dad?"
"He bought the farm yesterday,"
Junior said, just as calmly
as one talking about the weather.
Bought the farm? How did that come
to mean kicking the bucket?
Everybody knows that
kicking the bucket and buying the farm
mean the same thing.
Kicking a bucket and buying a farm
at the same time would kill anybody.
"I'm sorry to hear that, Junior."
Actually, you're not sorry. In fact
the news gave you a jolt of vigor:
Well, I outlived that bastard.
"It was so sudden," Junior said.
He held the steering wheel
in a kind of caress.

Junior's only emotion
at the moment was glee
at the thought of inheriting
an almost new truck.
The grief would come later.

The Contrarian Voice

Munch on a Village Store grinder
while you imagine Wife
standing at the sink
and gazing out the window
at her bird feeder,
just as she had done in life.
Tell her how sad you are:
connections and conniption fits
that enriched your life,
the Centenarian's stewpot,
involuntarily memorized glimpses
of trees, stonewalls, ledges,
old mossy gravestones,
fences and hosses and cows
and chickens and porcupines
and deer and skunks and woodchucks
and beavers and squirrels,
gray and red, and damn raccoons
and screeching foxes
and screechier fisher cats
and owls, eagles, and the little ones
at the bird feeder whose names
you never bothered to learn,
and once in a while a coyote,
couple times a bear, bobcats,

Saturday morning yard sales,
old tools at Ike's Flea Market, junk cars,
rides to the dump with the son
when he was a boy,
your mechanic's pit that the son
helped you dig when he was a boy,
before he disowned the likes of you,
the sky over your property,
town meetings, disasters
in the son ("Son, son,
why did you change your name?"),
daughters that you could do little for,
Daddy, I want to swing, push me,
you start them off,
release them, watch them,
on their own now,
pumping the swing, pumping, pumping,
leaping from the greatest height
into the chasm of their destinies—
you understand now, don't you, Octogenarian.
"Yes, once the girl children
can pump the swing for themselves
the male parent is no longer necessary."
Bees, dragonflies, ants, nightcrawlers,
even black flies.

"Yes, even you evil ones.
Home, not the same without you, darlin'."
The worst of it, Octogenarian,
is that the fire that kept you stoked
all these decades
to shield your fears
only produced a wheelbarrow
full of smoke
and has died to embers.
The figure of Wife fades,
and without it loneliness
envelops you,
a kind of suffocating protection.
"Like a poncho
in a foxhole
on a rainy night
in war."

What is it about you, Octogenarian,
that sign you put up,
Welcome to Re In Car Nation?
"I love the startling shapes,
textures brought on by time,
paint losing struggle with air,
incursions of plant life

in the crannies of stressed
and distressed metal,
patterns and play of light
made by smashed glass,
the fading from something to nothing,
the aura of the former owners
glowing in a half halo
around the junk cars.
I like rust, I like dead-end streets,
I like a break
in a Jack Landry curveball,
I like cracks in the pavement."
So what? You hurt people.
"My loved ones mainly,
though not on purpose."
But you hurt them.

When you were young,
you had a nice set of rights and wrongs.
"Like wrenches hanging over the workbench."
You got older, you got worn,
you saw *this* become *that* and *that* become *this*
and came to realize that a man always believes
he's living his life right today,
even if he was wrong ten years ago;
he gets forgetful about the joys of youth

and fretful about the despairs;
he comes to be a good judge of men and weather,
which makes him see the futility of trusting either;
he gets atheistic, and that makes him lonely;
he gets tired of doing the chores
and cranky when there is nothing to do;
he gets no thrill from pretties, no disgust from uglies—
a sunset and a flapdoodle, all the same.
White birch logs cut with a band saw
and put through machines
to make Scrabble tiles
to be stamped with letters,
which would be arranged
on game boards to make words
that would be scattered by a cat
and rearranged into a pattern
and questioned on the basis
of their authenticity
and so on until the human epoch
crashes into a great stillness:
that's your end, Octogenarian.
No fire, no ice, just stillness,
which gets the many-letter bonus
but whose individual letters
are worth only a point each
on Wife's Scrabble board,

which she played alone because
you didn't like losing
and would not indulge her and,
face it, didn't know that many words
to spell. Husband, Wife had said,
"correctly" does not have
a "wreck" in it.

You never made big money.
"But earned what I got."
Not hard to do when it's not much.
You only formed two worthwhile friendships.
"Yes, Ollie Jordan and Cooty Patterson."
A reprobate and a hermit,
neither Jeffersonian nor Belichickian patriots.
"Served my country best I could,
worked, worked, worked to build
the country best I could."
Failed.
"Hunted the whitetail deer,
think maybe hunting is inherited
like a serious overbite."
You married too young.
"But stayed together."
You never really got to know her.
"But produced healthy children."

Except too many.

"That last one, a surprise, a doozy."

A doozy? What is a doozy?

"A doozy is a daughter
singing startling and sweet
as boiling maple sap
spilled on fresh snow."

Ache of her loss, a guilt,
a feeling you resist.

"I don't respect guilt-riders."

But there it is, Octogenarian, a guilt.

"Smoked the Camel with great pleasure.
Gave up the Camel."

Not soon enough to save Wife—
secondhand smoke.

"The second hand of my watch is ticking."

The second hand of your death
is calling you
into the gloom of dark matter, no?

"Yes, I admit it.
Least you could do, Voice,
is let me forget."

A man can look neither to the past
nor to the future, because ... because?

"There is no such thing as time."

That's right.

The only legit questions are found
in the pauses between changes.
Calls for immediate action.
The now-whats.
Your son got it right
with that word you can't pronounce,
the i-n-t-e-r-s-t-i-c-e-s.
"Oh, shut up!"
Will not. Listen to me:
Do not dwell on conditions
that presume a flow of time—

hope, yearning, nostalgia, regret.
You told the world
you named yourself after an elm tree,
which was a lie,
and then somebody cut the tree down
to shame you.
"But I found it buried in a sandbank."
Bring your shame to a sawmill,
make boards, erect a casket,
lie in it during that long intermission.
Can you feel it—your grave?
Petrifying with your tree, tree to stone,
man to stone, monument to your shame?
Thing about a sandbank
is that it visibly changes.

What you see today is not
what you get tomorrow.
It is like watching the evolution
of a celestial body speeded up.
Aging is like that.
This sandbank is telling you there ain't no God.

Go to bed, Octogenarian, dream:
If *gnaw* is spelled g-n-a-w on Wife's board,
which you know to be true because she looked it up,
why isn't *north* spelled g-n-a-w-t-h?
"Gnawth, gnawth, gnawth."
Talking in your sleep again.
"Do me a favor, Voice, stay out of my dreams."
Look at you, Octogenarian,
trying to tap tap tap an e-mail
to Sane Daughter in South Texas.
"I have much to say."
But?
"I don't want to start a family avalanche."
Tell Sane Daughter you discovered
who cut your elm tree
but for reasons unknown.
Tell her your plan
to build your own coffin.
Apologize to her for being a bad father.

Tap tap tap, "Cold, wind from the gnawth.
See you later."
Click.
Send.
E-mail travels around the world,
into space and beyond in that realm
where elements are recycled into stars.
Saint Peter, cranky gatekeeper of Catholic heaven
and frequent lurker on the Internet,
intercepts message to Sane Daughter.
Checks it off as a venial sin
and files it in the database.
Saint Peter is tired. This job is a lot of work.
Slips a note in the Judgment Day Suggestion Box:
How about an honorable mention
for the lab mice who did more
for the species who enslaved them
than the species did for themselves?

Your offspring are ashamed of you,
Octogenarian. Get out of the way—
preferably, die;
they're going to kill you anyway
with their robots.
What do you prefer, Octogenarian,
lethal injection, hanging,

firing squad,
flattened by a steamroller?
"There are no steamrollers anymore;
they all run on diesel."
Just a manure of speaking.
"Yeah, well, everything is
a manure of speaking.
You can't say
nothing without it meaning something
you don't want it to mean
or don't even know you said."
Words corrupt everybody, Octogenarian.
What you think you know
is all a big pile
of manures of speaking.
You don't have a prayer.
"I don't have a prayer."

Saint Peter doesn't have a prayer,
so he checks the historical record,
bumps his forehead with his palm,
and calls out in Octogenarian's voice,
talking in his sleep,
"Jesus, I get it now:
the ones with no education,
the ones who made mistakes in youth

and paid for them over a lifetime,
the ones who built the idiot pyramids,
and the useless cathedrals,
and that stupid wall in China,
who sawed the Scrabble tiles,
who mined the coal and ran the looms,
who built literally everything,
the ones who slung the hash
and wiped the bottoms of the babies
and the old people in those prisons
they call nursing homes,
and who appeared in apparitions in the minds
of soldiers calling for their mothers
as they lay bleeding out on the battlefield,
and who fucked the bosses to save us all—
they are all fucked.
And fucked again.
And fucked over.
And fucked forever,
us, the working people."